A Bluenose Twelve Days of Christmas

Bruce Munn
2013.

A Bluenose Twelve Days of Christmas

BRUCE NUNN

Illustrations by
DORETTA GROENENDYK

NIMBUS
PUBLISHING

Nimbus Publishing Limited
3731 Mackintosh St, Halifax, NS B3K 5A5
(902) 455-4286 nimbus.ca

Printed and bound in China

Author photo: John Calder

Library and Archives Canada Cataloguing in Publication

Nunn, Bruce
A Bluenose : twelve days of Christmas / Bruce
Nunn, author ; Doretta Groenendyk, illustrator.
ISBN 978-1-55109-938-5

1. Bluenose (Ship)—Juvenile poetry. I. Groenendyk, Doretta II. Title.

PS8577.U5485B58 2012   jC811'.6   C2012-903670-6

Nimbus Publishing acknowledges the financial support for its publishing
activities from the Government of Canada through the Canada Book Fund
(CBF) and the Canada Council for the Arts, and from the Province of Nova
Scotia through the Department of Communities, Culture and Heritage.

For Nova Scotians everywhere who know
the many gifts this *Bluenose* province has to
give. Merry Christmas.
—B. N.

For David, Izra, Reilly and Jasper
—D. G.

On the first day of Christmas,
My true love gave to me...
A Bluenose in at Pier Three.

On the second day of Christmas,
My true love gave to me...
Two fiddle tunes
And a Bluenose in at Pier Three.

2

On the third day of Christmas,
My true love gave to me...
Three lobster traps
Two fiddle tunes
And a Bluenose in at Pier Three.

On the fourth day of Christmas,
My true love gave to me...
Four coal seams
Three lobster traps
Two fiddle tunes
And a Bluenose in at Pier Three.

6

On the fifth day of Christmas,
My true love gave to me...
Five Highland flings

Four coal seams
Three lobster traps
Two fiddle tunes
And a Bluenose in at Pier Three.

On the sixth day of Christmas,
My true love gave to me...
Six boats-a-fishing

Five Highland flings

Four coal seams
Three lobster traps
Two fiddle tunes
And a Bluenose in at Pier Three.

On the seventh day of Christmas,
My true love gave to me...
Seven salmon swimming
Six boats-a-fishing

Five Highland flings

Four coal seams
Three lobster traps
Two fiddle tunes
And a Bluenose in at Pier Three.

On the eighth day of Christmas,
My true love gave to me...
Eight tides-a-turning
Seven salmon swimming
Six boats-a-fishing

Five Highland flings

Four coal seams
Three lobster traps
Two fiddle tunes
And a Bluenose in at Pier Three.

On the ninth day of Christmas,
My true love gave to me...
Nine crafters hooking
Eight tides-a-turning
Seven salmon swimming
Six boats-a-fishing

Five Highland flings

Four coal seams
Three lobster traps
Two fiddle tunes
And a Bluenose in at Pier Three.

On the tenth day of Christmas,
My true love gave to me...
Ten lights-a-keeping
Nine crafters hooking
Eight tides-a-turning
Seven salmon swimming
Six boats-a-fishing

Five Highland flings

Four coal seams
Three lobster traps
Two fiddle tunes
And a Bluenose in at Pier Three.

On the eleventh day of Christmas,
My true love gave to me...
Eleven plovers piping
Ten lights-a-keeping
Nine crafters hooking
Eight tides-a-turning
Seven salmon swimming
Six boats-a-fishing

Five Highland flings

Four coal seams
Three lobster traps
Two fiddle tunes
And a Bluenose in at Pier Three.

21

On the twelfth day of Christmas,
My true love gave to me...
Twelve drummers drumming
Eleven plovers piping
Ten lights-a-keeping
Nine crafters hooking
Eight tides-a-turning
Seven salmon swimming
Six boats-a-fishing

Five Highland flings

Four coal seams
Three lobster traps
Two fiddle tunes
And a Bluenose in at Pier Three!

22

Lyrics of the traditional Twelve Days of Christmas

On the first day of Christmas,
my true love gave to me...
A partridge in a pear tree.

On the second day of Christmas,
my true love gave to me...
Two turtle doves,
And a partridge in a pear tree.

On the third day of Christmas,
my true love gave to me...
Three French hens,
Two turtle doves,
And a partridge in a pear tree.

On the fourth day of Christmas,
my true love gave to me...
Four calling birds,
Three French hens,
Two turtle doves,
And a partridge in a pear tree.

On the fifth day of Christmas,
my true love gave to me...
Five golden rings,
Four calling birds,
Three French hens,
Two turtle doves,
And a partridge in a pear tree.

On the sixth day of Christmas,
my true love gave to me...
Six geese a-laying,
Five golden rings,
Four calling birds,
Three French hens,
Two turtle doves,
And a partridge in a pear tree.

On the seventh day of Christmas,
my true love gave to me...
Seven swans a-swimming,
Six geese a-laying,
Five golden rings,
Four calling birds,
Three French hens,
Two turtle doves,
And a partridge in a pear tree.

On the eighth day of Christmas,
my true love gave to me...
Eight maids a-milking,
Seven swans a-swimming,
Six geese a-laying,
Five golden rings,
Four calling birds,
Three French hens,
Two turtle doves,
And a partridge in a pear tree.

On the ninth day of Christmas,
my true love gave to me...
Nine ladies dancing,
Eight maids a-milking,
Seven swans a-swimming,
Six geese a-laying,
Five golden rings,
Four calling birds,
Three French hens,
Two turtle doves,
And a partridge in a pear tree.

On the tenth day of Christmas,
my true love gave to me...
Ten lords a-leaping,
Nine ladies dancing,
Eight maids a-milking,
Seven swans a-swimming,
Six geese a-laying,
Five golden rings,
Four calling birds,
Three French hens,
Two turtle doves,
And a partridge in a pear tree.

On the eleventh day of Christmas,
my true love gave to me...
Eleven pipers piping,
Ten lords a-leaping,
Nine ladies dancing,
Eight maids a-milking,
Seven swans a-swimming,
Six geese a-laying,
Five golden rings,
Four calling birds,
Three French hens,
Two turtle doves,
And a partridge in a pear tree.

On the twelfth day of Christmas,
my true love gave to me...
Twelve drummers drumming,
Eleven pipers piping,
Ten lords a-leaping,
Nine ladies dancing,
Eight maids a-milking,
Seven swans a-swimming,
Six geese a-laying,
Five golden rings,
Four calling birds,
Three French hens,
Two turtle doves,
And a partridge in a pear tree!